ADVENTURES IN CULTURE

COOKING
AROUND THE WORLD

By Jeff Sferazza

Gareth Stevens
PUBLISHING

T0004663

Please visit our website, www.garethstevens.com. For a free color catalog of all our high-quality books, call toll free 1-800-542-2595 or fax 1-877-542-2596.

Cataloging-in-Publication Data

Names: Sferazza, Jeff.
Title: Cooking around the world / Jeff Sferazza.
Description: New York : Gareth Stevens Publishing, 2019. | Series: Adventures in culture | Includes glossary and index.
Identifiers: LCCN ISBN 9781538218617 (pbk.) | ISBN 9781538218594 (library bound) | ISBN 9781538218624 (6 pack)
Subjects: LCSH: Food–Juvenile literature. | Food habits–Juvenile literature. | Food habits–Cross-cultural studies–Juvenile literature.
Classification: LCC TX353.S44 2019 | DDC 641.3–dc23

Published in 2019 by
Gareth Stevens Publishing
111 East 14th Street, Suite 349
New York, NY 10003

Copyright © 2019 Gareth Stevens Publishing

Designer: Katelyn E. Reynolds
Editor: Meta Manchester

Photo credits: Cover, p. 1 LunaseeStudios/Shutterstock.com; pp. 2–24 (background texture) Flas100/Shutterstock.com; p. 5 George Pachantouris/Moment/Getty Images; p. 7 Trial/Shutterstock.com; p. 9 Carolina Arroyo/Shutterstock.com; p. 11 Paolo Rossetti/arabianEye/Getty Images; p. 13 Akira Kaede/Stockbyte/Getty Images; p. 15 c.H/Thehoffmanns/Wikipedia.org; p. 17 Chris Jackson/Getty Images; p. 19 mc559 (http://flickr.com/photos/87807550@N00/)/ Creative Commons Attribution-Share Alike 2.0 Generic (https://creativecommons.org/licenses/by-sa/2.0/deed.en)/Wikipedia.org; p. 21 Hill Street Studios/Blend Images/Getty Images.

All rights reserved. No part of this book may be reproduced in any form without permission in writing from the publisher, except by a reviewer.

Printed in the United States of America

CPSIA compliance information: Batch #CS18GS: For further information contact Gareth Stevens, New York, New York at 1-800-542-2595.

CONTENTS

Boldface words appear in the glossary.

The Joy of Cooking

With so many different **cultures** on Earth, you might be surprised to hear that some ways of cooking happen almost everywhere. After all, many cultures have pots, pans, and ovens. But some ways of cooking are like no other!

Steaming

For thousands of years, Chinese cooking has used **steam** baskets made of bamboo. These baskets are stacked on top of each other during cooking. The food needing the most cooking is put in the bottom basket, closest to the boiling water.

Tamales

Tamales are a special holiday treat in Central and South America. To make tamales, special corn **dough** is filled with cheese, meat, vegetables, or spicy peppers called chilis. They're then **wrapped** in corn **husks** or banana leaves and steamed or cooked over a fire.

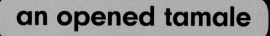
an opened tamale

9

Potjie Pots

South African potjie (POY-KEE) pots are iron pots with heavy lids, round bottoms, and three legs. They're used for cooking food over hot coals, which can be moved closer if more heat is needed. Potjie is like stew, but it's never stirred while it's cooking!

11

Iroris

Iroris are square fire pits that were once found inside some Japanese homes. It was like having a campfire in the middle of your house! Iroris gave warmth, light, and heat for cooking. Today, they're mostly found in **traditional** restaurants.

13

Schwenkers

In Germany, some people cook with swinging **grills** called schwenkers. Schwenkers are hung over coals using three-legged stands. They're kept swinging so the food cooks evenly. The type of pork that's traditionally cooked on these grills is also called "schwenker."

15

Hangis

In New Zealand, the Maori people cook in underground ovens called hangis. Food is put on top of large, hot rocks inside a hangi. **Layers** of wet cloths and dirt are then placed on top. This makes steam that cooks the food!

Hot Sand Frying

In China and India, people called street vendors cook and sell food right on the street. They fry nuts in large pans filled with black sand. The pans are heated, and the hot sand cooks the nuts. The nuts are then picked out and sold!

chestnuts frying in black sand

19

Get Cooking!

People around the world cook their food in many ways. But everyone has one thing in common—we all need to eat! You can learn more about cooking around the world by taking a cooking class for kids. What tasty foods will you cook first?

GLOSSARY

culture: the beliefs and ways of life of a group of people

dough: a mix of flour and water

grill: a metal frame used to cook food over fire

husk: a thin, dry layer that covers some fruits and seeds

layer: one thickness of something lying over or under another

steam: water turned into vapor by boiling

traditional: having to do with long-practiced ways of life

wrap: to cover something by folding material around it

FOR MORE INFORMATION

BOOKS

Barghoorn, Linda. *Foods in Different Places*. New York, NY: Crabtree Publishing Company, 2016.

Davies, Monika. *Art and Culture: Desserts Around the World*. Huntington Beach, CA: Teacher Created Materials, 2017.

Petrie, Kristin. *Food Culture: Celebrating Diverse Traditions*. Edina, MN: ABDO, 2012.

WEBSITES

Cultures for Kids
cultureforkids.exploreandmore.org/
Click on the map to explore new cultures right from your home.

Kid World Citizen
kidworldcitizen.org/category/food/
Check out fun recipes and crafts from around the world.

Publisher's note to educators and parents: Our editors have carefully reviewed these websites to ensure that they are suitable for students. Many websites change frequently, however, and we cannot guarantee that a site's future contents will continue to meet our high standards of quality and educational value. Be advised that students should be closely supervised whenever they access the internet.

INDEX